OTHER WAYS

OTHER WAYS

RESCUING THE CHURCH FROM PHAROAH
and Other Poems

by
PETER KEESE

RESOURCE *Publications* • Eugene, Oregon

OTHER WAYS
Rescuing the Church from Pharoah and Other Poems

Copyright © 2024 Peter Keese. All rights reserved. Except for brief quotations in critical publications or reviews, no part of this book may be reproduced in any manner without prior written permission from the publisher. Write: Permissions, Wipf and Stock Publishers, 199 W. 8th Ave., Suite 3, Eugene, OR 97401.

Resource Publications
An Imprint of Wipf and Stock Publishers
199 W. 8th Ave., Suite 3
Eugene, OR 97401

www.wipfandstock.com

PAPERBACK ISBN: 979-8-3852-1244-6
HARDCOVER ISBN: 979-8-3852-1245-3
EBOOK ISBN: 979-8-3852-1246-0

VERSION NUMBER 021424

Contents

Trees | 1
Dead and Alive | 3
A Letter to Mother Church | 5
Tears | 9
Ode to St. Augustine | 11
Occam's Razor | 13
Keeping Score* | 17
Tell Old Pharaoh | 18
Jesus Was a Healthy Boy | 19
Sin | 21
Jerusalem Jerusalem | 22
The Church's Prayer | 25
With Apologies to Emily | 26
What We Have Here is a Failure to Imagine | 29
Executioner's Lament | 31
Innocent | 32
Alan* | 33
Let it Be | 34
The Commandment | 36
A Sea of Ignorance | 37
Don't Ask | 38

Serious | 39
At the Beach | 40
Graced | 41
I Almost Missed It | 43
Wedding | 44
Meditation | 46
Vladimir | 48
OTOH | 49
Words Play | 50
WAR | 51
Gratitude | 54
Kind | 55
A Dream | 56
Anthony Dominick Benedetto Died Today | 57
My Creed | 58
The Angriest Man in Brooklyn | 59
Genius | 60
Ism | 61
The garden | 63
Grits | 65
Prevenient | 66
Weather | 67
Naked Greed | 68

The Struggle | 69
The Buddha Paradox | 70
Similar | 71
The Super Blue Moon | 72
The Secret | 73
Quantum Physics | 74
Fall Haiku | 75
Nakedness Revisited | 76
Shawn | 77
The Heaven I Don't Believe In | 78
Quantum Philosophy | 79
East and West | 81
He and She | 82
Dumbass | 83
Peace | 84
Connection | 86

The Dog that Did Not Bark | 88
Poetry | 90
A Funny Thing Happened on the Way | 91
Fish | 92
Mortal | 94
Life | 95
Gift | 96
The Horror | 99
Mink | 100
Three Red Tomatoes | 101
TS Eliot Revisited | 102
Meeting | 104
How it All Started | 105
How It Ends | 107

Trees

It is a normal event, I guess
the chlorophyll in recess
our green once vibrant and bright
fades now into the night

we belonged—a community
with common purpose
and a common language
we were attached
leaf to branch
branch to limb
limb to trunk
we were alive
we danced together
in the wind
and suffered together
in the rain and cold
we belonged to one another
green alive connected

so is our time now past?
our life fading fast?
we've been dropped off
disconnected

the young ones yet attached
mistake our grounded condition
for death—for nonbeing
we commiserate

Other Ways

amongst ourselves
and seek to demonstrate
that we are yet
somebody

fallen leaves rich compost,
soil enhanced trees healthy
life not lost
perhaps more wealthy
we enrich the roots

Dead and Alive

I've been lying here
for many years
people think I'm dead
but there are no tears

and I'm not dead either!
all those muons, protons, neurons
jiggling around inside me
not to mention the
worms, beatles, ants
and the glorious hungry fungi
luxuriating in the decay
of my long fallen trunk

and it's decay*ing* not decay -
active—not otherwise
the grass grows around
and tickles my thighs
I laugh and we talk and play
all day

the human enterprise
to categorize
dead OR alive
is the way we think

dually

but I'm both

Other Ways

at once
one
alive
constantly jiggling
energetic

"The worms crawl in
the worms crawl out
the worms play pinochle
on my snout."

ha ha ha ha ha

A Letter to Mother Church

she's my mother,
the Church.
I can do no other
but search
beyond love/hate for
real appreciation and
full acclamation
and thanks
for the gift

baptism before memory
awe majesty order
power father's approval
mother's nurture

A certain snobbery yes
theology osmotic
bible spasmotic
(we're episcopalians, you know)

episcopalian—lifelong
christian more cultural
than convicted
and besides
I like the club

in my early thirties, a priest
letter from natal mother:
"infant fever, you near died

Other Ways

I promised you to God
if you survived"
news to me—spooky

sixty plus years
pretending
to be a priest
and being a priest
in spite of pretense

when they first called me Father
I look around to see
who they were talking to
sixty years it can be
sometimes true
that I possess
the power to bless

"Wake up, Son", she says
"you have to go to church"

I don't want to

"you have to"

why

"because you are
the rector"

bada, bada, bing

diagnosis
Peter has
Priest disease.

A Letter to Mother Church

is it fatal
damn near
what is it
taking theology
seriously

it has taken him
eighty plus years
to see what
the *laos* reveres
until we devise
to convince them
otherwise

it is not the theology
it is belonging
to the club

is that a bad thing
well, yes and no
like every club
it sings its virtues
like every club
it sees no blemish
or hides lest it diminish
its shining glory

mother sends me off
to finishing school
unblemished is the plan
by any hint or scan
of worldly vice
which might corrupt
and interrupt
my path to sweet
perfection

Other Ways

a-soldiering, I'd learn to swear
on soldier's leave I'd compare
my tender unsullied innocence
with lives that hint deep and dense
musky forests with that apple
I'd eat and then I'd know...

who told you that was wicked
who said it is destruction
why, Mom, it is your construction
designed to protect
from risk of hurt in
that dangerous
workaday world

Tears

I've finally figured it out
why I have to drag myself
to church

church doesn't make me cry
that's why

a violin piece or Mozart
that's the kind of art
that makes me cry

a majestic sonata
a beautiful cantata
beyond the capacity
of words

or the beautiful child
dancing in the aisle
evokes my smile
and tears of joy

rarely the words
it's the music and dance
as the swoop of the birds
makes the heart prance
and swing and play
perhaps even pray
a joyous thanks

Other Ways

oh, and it does make me laugh
but not liturgical plan
when that beautiful moppet
escaped mom's clutch
and she could not stop it
we all laughed with such
delight

the solemn high mass
too fancy to pass
muster
with the common cluster
wanting the jug and the loaf
and the song and the dance
and the tears and the laughter
that humans advance

liturgical rehearsal itself
tends against the wealth
of the tears and the laughter
and the joy and the dance

greyhound station master
speaks only faster
but not more elegant than
the average priest celebrant

I wonder—do you
how it can be that
the Phantom is ever new
fresh each performance
should the liturgy be, too?

is the tug at the heart-strings
the tears and the laughter
the appropriate things
that we should be after?

Ode to St. Augustine

depraved fallen world original sin
who prescribed this awful din
why none other than Augustin

gloom despair and awful misery
good ol Augie posed these three
"original sin" his original phrase
prescribing for us a terrible phase

unless. . .

salvation which comes from above
depends on our bow to the bountiful dove
groveling humbling repenting we cry
a miserable sinner from birth am I

rescue and redemption come only from YOU
good ol Augie concocted this stew.
who is this Augie, anyhow
and why treat him with a bow

why cause the church has said it's so
and proclaims a savior come below
from godly throne in heaven above
to cleanse us with self-offering love

in the person of Jesus, god's only son
who then kills his boy and thus has won
eternal victory for this mortal crowd

Other Ways

reminding us that we be not proud
it's his not ours—we're God endowed
with loving life—His not ours

Augie's rule we're conceived in sin
it is our very own origin

oh Augie Augie our seminal book
see Genesis one—take a look
there the original is declared to be
good—very good—for all to see

maybe, Augie, you need therapy.

Occam's Razor

he is worth following, this man
lots of stories about him
from long back
when biographical details
were lacking

so we really know little and
surmise a lot.
we think he valued people
as people, one by one.
we think he thought love was
what it is all about

we think he was rabbinical
in the way he taught
—with wisdom and authority
recalling the Jewish ethos
love your neighbor
welcome the stranger
feed the hungry
heal the sick

we think he instructed us
to follow him
in this ethos,
loving universally,
as he taught

do not

Other Ways

the Buddhists
the Hindus
the Sikhs
the Jains
the Taoists
the Methodists
the Muslims
the mystics
the Baptists
the Catholics
the philosophers
even the Episcopalians
and "non-religious"
do they not all counsel
the very same

Occam is not alone
in saying that
the least complicated
or cluttered
is often the truest

the ethos of love is
as they say
simple but not easy
of accomplishment

soon those who
purported to follow
the rabbi
decided to
worship him instead

somehow **_HIS_**
"Sacrifice"

Occam's Razor

his body and blood
becomes our object
of worship

and he has come
to signify a talisman to
ward off evil
think goats scaped
or crucifix

he, no longer one of us
but **_GOD_**
is our hero
our savior
he has done the work
we worship HIM

We are not responsible
helpless we are caught
enslaved in sin

we don't follow him on
Sunday morning we grovel
and our preachers assure us
week upon week
that we are right
poor helpess supplicants
to depend only on him

****

Occam suggests that
Jesus _as savior_ is
an unneccesary element
it complicates clutters obfuscates

Other Ways

the message of love

That like Abraham L. Ghandi MLK
he is an exemplar
not a savior

Keeping Score*

Do you reckon he really meant
that so as to pay the rent
four hundred and ninety times
is the absolute requirement

What if death comes at 489
will I have to pay a fine
or be forever excluded

Outcomes desired are these—his call
is feed clothe visit heal them all
And what about church and my prayers
feeding and such IS church he declares

Well, again, how many
prayers, healings and all is aplenty
and what is the measure to apply
is there a precise number to satisfy
the outcomes

seven times seven
seventy times seven
what is the right leaven

and how will I know

*Matthew 18:21

Tell Old Pharaoh

maybe I'm just an old grump
with decidedly contrarian leaning
my complaints about church may trump
the good news at the core of my meaning

the problem begins right here
the news is not good but mixed,
it is good only when you make it so

the news is here for you to see
you have all the power
and you are free

the current Christian message
gives god all the credit
which only means you edit
yourself out of the picture –
powerless—you disappear

so which is it to be -
free agent and responsibility
or non-entity

a trick question
you have no choice
except to deny or
claim your voice

"Go down, Moses
way down in Egypt land
tell old Pharaoh
to let my people go."

Jesus Was a Healthy Boy

Jesus was a healthy boy
at age fourteen he found the joy
and the pleasure of masturbation
and maybe even in a later station
of life the joys of carnal knowledge

or was he a sexist or maybe queer
the faithful twelve he held dear—
all male and he was ready to ditch
that foreign woman he called bitch

racist sexist male supremist
but oh boy could he spin a tale
and draw a crowd and regale
them with powerful eloquence

he knew the Bible and impressed
the wise men in the temple
by his distillation of the simple
message of their own prophets
feed the hungry prisoners free
clothe the naked make blind see

in time there came a throng
of those who saw him as king
it is not clear that he went along
but his message had the ring
of rebellion to the Roman power
they executed him but. . .

Other Ways

    the message has continued to flower

      is it blasphemy, as you may fear
    that I dare suggest in words so clear
     that he was just a normal male
      is it so far beyond the pale
      to think that even you or me
     might also set the people free

Sin

we're all infected
as was detected
by Augustine

he's right so far

but he thinks the cure
the only thing sure
is God's action

by which

we're off the hook
his shepherd's crook
is around his own son's neck

so we're all set free
it's his responsibility.

we're in the kingdom
we're god's own
we thank god that we
are not like them

Jerusalem Jerusalem

"Jerusalem! Jerusalem!
murderer of prophets
how often I've ached
to embrace your children
the way a hen gathers
her chicks under her wings
and you wouldn't let me"[1]

this brief piece is attributed to Jesus
I thought of it this morning
as I went into deep mourning
listening to the sermon

text—owner of the vineyard
sends to gather the fruit
workers won't provide it.[2]

preacher left me dumbfounded
I was astounded
and truly saddened
initially maddened
at his seeming failure
to understand the message

which is so very simple
with no flaw or wrinkle
Jesus is just repeating

1. Matthew 23:37
2. Matthew 21:33-46

JERUSALEM JERUSALEM

once again completing
what Isaiah and others
had already said

namely

you wise men of your nation
claiming exalted station
as leaders of your people
and obedient to god's command
have utterly failed

preacher says it is about
god's ownership of the vineyard
assuring us of the comfort
of knowing we are safe and loved
faith in god's sovereignty
is the whole of his interpretation

I think he is mistaken

Jesus is saying
to christians gathered
each Sunday morning

you think that by repeating rote
the words of your eucharist
and your standard intercessions
and confessions you are safe
in god's kingdom

you are not

depending on the law alone
no matter how meticulous
is simple and ridiculous

Other Ways

I have sent to see the fruit
how many hungry have you fed
how many homeless have you led
to home
how many blind see
how many prisoners free

"I hate, I despise your feast days,
and I do not savor
your sacred assemblies."[3]

Oh Jerusalem Jerusalem

3. Amos 5:21

The Church's Prayer

    thank you, Lord, that
    I am not like those others
      I tithe and I pray
      they only prey

        sin
       I see it
      I know it
    I recognize it. . .

      in them

    thank you Lord
    that I am not like them
     I'm a Christian
    in Church every Sunday

    Jesus is my talisman

With Apologies to Emily

we're different, and you
we'll make you different too

the church's message hiding
beneath her smiling face
you should not be abiding
at the ordinary pace

of sinful life as you are
you must be saved
from your situation far
from your current depravity
to become a heavenly star

how dreary to be sinful
what a sad condition
to spend your livelong days
your only end perdition

we'll polish you up
give a shiny patina
we'll sing and pray
so all will say
she's one of us
no spot or blemish.

but Mother. . .

pardon me but

With Apologies to Emily

  here's where you failed
  you kept me unassailed
   by queers and
  married couples impaled
  on deep disagreements
    unspoken
   by wars and whores
  and many things unsavory
'be nice' the guiding flavoring

nice—*ne scire*=not to know

   but I do know
   I'm not nice Mother
what shall I do with these other
   impulses dark hidden
   unpolished blemishes

   Does Mother's club
    really require
    that I retire
     or
   at least disguise
   to hide from eyes
   my hate my greed
   my envy my lust
  is it really that I must
    be cleansed

   or is it perhaps
  that our only lapse is
  that stuff seems evil
  when we keep it dark

  what if I give them light
  and hug them tight

Other Ways

might greed serve good
and lust serve love

so, thank you no
I think I'll go
amongst my kind
and there I'll find
companions plenty

besmirched and smudged
yet sans the drudge -
the burden of toting
the unbearable weight of
perfection

The surprising paradox
so unorthodox
and what you won't allow
is to see how

*fault—***is**—*the perfection.*

O felix culpa

What We Have Here is a Failure to Imagine

(inspired by a recent visit to the Legacy Museum, Montgomery, Alabama)

only heads are visible
the enslaved, drowning
in the angry sea
how can we
have been
so cruel

not I
never
it is not in me
I can't imagine

Peter, my best friend
you will betray me
even before the rooster
can see

not I
never
it is not in me
I can't imagine

Sheriff Tom Coleman
shot young Jon Daniels

not I
never
it is not in me

Other Ways

I can't imagine

those unutterably stupid
unfeeling Republicans
I hate them every one
I would never
treat anyone
the way they do

not I
never
it is not in me
I can't imagine

Executioner's Lament

I prepare his arm
to avoid any harm
find the right line
the needle so fine

this med calms
and this one balms
and this one—

this one stops it all

BAM

never mind it's all ok
not mine to say
but simply to do
and not to rue
the state's command

eye for eye says the book
does that let me off the hook?
Bible says, state commands
surely that looses the bands
of my guilt

but who tonight will bed with me
and help me wrest my conscience free
from such a terrible plan
I will have killed a man

Innocent

Billy Budd was not bad
he was said to be a charming lad
winsome handsome sweet
and innocent

beloved by most
darkly envied by one
who began to boast
that he has begun
to suspect Billy Budd
of mutiny

Billy's dismay overwhelmed
he could not speak
surprised himself with
a mighty blow to wreak
murder on the man

Billy Budd was hanged
for murder

some say it was
his innocence
that did him in
that in a sense
if he had but known—
befriended—his
murderer—
it would not have
overwhelmed him

Alan*

The code is broken
Enigma is no longer

"*The convoy is marked
For attack*

*My brother is on the ship
we must warn them*"

NO!

"*Hundreds will die
without warning*"

Yes, and thousands
will die
if <u>they</u> know
that <u>we</u> know
the code

"*You are acting like God*"

I am

---

*Alan Turing 'invented' the computer which helped to break the German code, Enigma

Let it Be

you have work to do:
struggle. . .
with faith
and doubt

that's what
the preacher said

he said
struggling is
the way
to comprehend
and thus overcome
doubt
you have to
work at it

maybe so. . .
it seems to be
the Western way
to see
"Come Labor On. . ."
says the hymn

if you work hard
you may grasp the full
beauty of
the Grand Canyon
he said

Let it Be

work grasp
struggle wrestle

or alternately

might you instead
let yourself *be*
comprehended

let it surround
consume
prehend you

let it be

let it be—
it comes to you
the beauty is there
surrounding

let it be

The Commandment

love your neighbor
as you love yourself
God says

a commandment ?
no
a simple description
of the way
it is

A Sea of Ignorance

I'm floating on a sea of ignorance, he said

fifteen or twenty years now
every Saturday morning we've met for
serious man-talk quantum theory
economics God and very rarely
any hint of frivolity

serious man-talk mostly above the neck
but today he mentions floating on that sea
and tells the most tender love story
revealing in the telling
that he knows that
the ignorance is just another way
to celebrate that life is so rich
though we'll never understand but
a tiny fraction...
we can luxuriate in that sea

Don't Ask

"don't ask how it can be",
says Feynman*
"nobody knows how it can be"

yet

everybody knows that God is male
that he wants us all to
worship him in the beauty of holiness
that he is
all wise
all powerful
all loving

how can this be—
is epistemic humility
required for us to see
that nobody knows

oh, woe is me—
no certainty
what shall I do
except to rue

or maybe rejoice
to give happy voice
to the beauty of floating
in the sea of ignorance

* Richard Feynman (1918-1988) was a noted Quantum scientist and teacher

Serious

I mean, I'm serious
about this
it is important enough
to be
delerious
about this

no foolin' around
no playing the clown
we have to get down
to being serious
about this

serious
I mean I'm serious
about this

a subject so profound
must never be drowned
in satire or such
the business is much
too serious

Archimedes was clever
he asked for big lever
to move the whole earth
this was not mirth

this was serious

we need to be
serious about this

At the Beach

(two summers after Helen's death)

dipping swerving
always in formation
as if dancing
heart-wrenchingly graceful

I sit on the sand and watch
the birds, and. . .

maybe nostalgizing
and idealizing
I'm in mind of
being married

as

always being in
formation

even
when
we weren't

at the beach

I miss her

Graced

graced with time
and aged so to focus
now attention as
not before

it is an hour before dark
for the first time this spring
I am sitting outside reading
a wonderful novel

but the grace is in listening
as never before
to the birds
talking

so many different voices
back and forth
are they talking and listening
I am listening

a tweet a chirp
a song a trill
staccato
and melody
a call an answer

it is still light but
dimming
less sound from the birds

Other Ways

do they get quiet with
the evening

then they start up again
but more quietly

dusk

I go inside

I Almost Missed It

OK—time to go in
so dutifully I
get up pick up my book
and then. . .

who says
who is this time-keeper

so I take my seat
look at the
leaves way up
caressing one another
sensual tender
dancing swaying

a long time entranced. . .

then the clouds
appear

sensual almost erotic
as they melt into
one another over
and over
soft gentle
lovers

I almost missed it

Wedding

two good men
ask me to bless their
marriage

I'm honored
but. . .
they want a
homily

I was only married
for 57 years
what do I know

then. . .

I looked at Helen's
wedding portrait
the other day

beautiful white gown
beautiful woman
then I noticed

she's looking sideways
with a glance that is
so invitingly impish

59 years and
I'd never noticed that

Wedding

in the picture
'til now

that woman
two and a half years
gone from this life
is still enriching me

that glance reminds me
of the never-ending
joy of discovering
the riches which
continue to reveal
themselves

you two will surprise
and delight each other
the rest of your lives,
discovering and flourishing in
the riches which
only gradually
over time
reveal themselves

Meditation

om—deep breaths
long exhales

Abraham –
no, not that one,
honest Abe
and Martin –
no, not that one,
MLK, Jr

but those others
belong too

and

Volodimir and
Vladimir
Xi and Mao
and Adolf
Joseph
both of them
and Genghis Khan

Sarah Rebecca,
Mary Mary Julian
Joan, Florence
and. . .

meditation –

Meditation

>breathing –
om

>oh — I see
I am breathing in meditation
I am inspiring and respiring
their breath

>and they mine

Vladimir

appears to me

what if I
could persuade
a million souls
to join the parade

to hold him in mind
our intent benign
and in our heart
so for our part
would be our plan
that the family of man
include him

as one of us

OTOH

with apologies to Harry*
we must always parry
the right hand
with the left

so tempted always
to declare and praise
the one true way
I'll not sway

on the other hand
strike up the band
I'll take my stand
on the other hand. . .

but biology prevails
and nothing avails
to deny that
dexter and sinister are
siblings

so, as they say
in show biz
put your hands
together

*Truman

Words Play

paradox

para dox
distinct from
right thinking

contradiction

speaking a contrary
about right thinking

distinct from what's right
or
is there another right

paradox

how can it be

exactly

WAR

on poverty and drugs
on cancer and thugs
we're against such sin
we're at war to win

pardon such doggerel
but some might say
war is not the only, and
maybe not the best way

to think about and
grapple with these ills

war enemies
hate killing
othering
divide and conquer
metaphor

Sun Tzu advises
keep your friends close
keep your enemies closer
is Jesus agreeing with Sun Tzu
in saying love your enemies

what might this mean
on Christmas Day in
1914 a spontaneous truce
broke out—soccer and comradery

Other Ways

the blokes and the huns
a brief embrace a day of
loving the enemy
some soldiers never forgot that
the best day they said

really can such be
cancer a companion boon
or addiction which soon
will take your life away
they are your friends

NA says befriending your
addict is the only way
AA says the same

was the frog wrong to befriend
the scorpion?

maybe this brief poem should
be titled "a riddle"
or
"a mystery"

hating your enemy it is said
is like you taking the poison
so that your enemy
will die

ask anyone who has
killed another in combat
how that worked out for them

WAR

embracing your enemy
unimaginable
and hating your enemy
will kill you

is the choice only
to die
at war
or
at peace

do we have a choice

it is all mystery

Gratitude

an attitude
the wings of a plane
set to maintain
steady ways
in turbulent days

thank you we say
at the close of the day
and as well at sunrise
so to keep our eyes

on the gift

Kind

I sit with him

he is not easy or calm
with himself
knows his flaws
continually gnaws
at his greed envy hate
pettiness—no abate

yet it comes to me
a voice

be kind to him

A Dream

whence she comes
I know not

just now she's here
pretty, slender, blonde
blue dress

she delights in me
in her eyes
there is no fault in me

we kiss
soft lips
eyes open
beautiful eyes

we walk
holding hands

her soft laugh
sparkles with yes

thanks

Anthony Dominick Benedetto Died Today

July 21, 2023

I left my heart
with my love Helen
when she died
two years ago

and on this day
she comes to me.
years ago we found our way
to hear Tony Bennett
we asked him to play
and sing
his signature melody

on this day
you come to me so
when I come home to you
beloved Helen
your golden sun
will shine for me

My Creed

universal life force
surrounds and inheres
energizes all
morally aware
all empowering
so that. . .
I can hate
or love
my choice
Truly

The Angriest Man in Brooklyn

I watched a movie on TV tonight
it was not a very good one.
it starred Robin Williams
I really like him
and it had lots of cute stuff but. . .
maybe it was that
it tried too hard to be profound

clunky device perhaps Robin plays a man
who believes he has just a few minutes to live
the griefs in his life—lost loves—he covers with rage
clunky perhaps but still. . .
here may be a profound thought
it is all always and only
and always about love and death
(Auden calls it Eros and dust)
that's it
watch any movie read any novel or poem
it's all about love and death
read the Bible read Shakespeare
it's about love and death
life is about love and death
only—that's all there is

Genius

Playing is such a joy
imagination is the ploy
Feynman is the name
he of considerable fame

genius is genetic, he says;
"you inherit it from your
children"

a giant in quantum physics
his intelligence is prodigious
humor-filled and delicious

imaginatively, playful like a child
he lectures on major aspects
of the quantum style
and laughs uproariously
all the while

this scientific genius going
office to office in Los Alamos
picking their locks

for fun

leaving his more serious colleagues

stunned

laughing uproariously
all the while

Ism

which is your favorite
I wish to savor it
so I'll know
which way to go
is it race or is it age
or is whiteness all the rage
or is it sex
is that the text

let's try this or maybe that
whichever one to bell the cat
and once we've attached the bell
we'll know who to send to. . .

but wait. . . these labels serve who
and what goal do they pursue

oh you're inflicted with racism
or maybe it's ageism or sexism
or worst of all your white supremism
there's no hope—you're afflicted with all

do we really need an ism
is it truly the best prism
by which to gauge
and declare with sage
wisdom your fatal cage

maybe human is the true 'affliction'

Other Ways

I like that—it's my conviction
that human describes me and you
I am one and you are too
let's try humanism

The garden

I'll take the back way
it's a pretty spring day
in no hurry to arrive
I'll enjoy the drive

dawdling along my lord,
how peaceful how serene
I round a curve my word
a beautiful garden green

and scaped with fruits
and vegetables and flowers
artfully placed among the bowers
I stop. . . my breath taken

exit the car
step to the fence
in the back corner far
I spot thence

in her little sun bonnet
with the ribbons upon it
the woman who tends
this beautiful sonnet

hello. . .hello, she kindly replies
I note the beauty that strikes my eyes
'a gorgeous work you

Other Ways

and the Lord have done'

hmphh..says she
what a sight to see
when the Lord
had it by himself

Grits

a yankee man
in a southern town
for breakfast

two eggs over light
and coffee out of sight
toast on the side
grits you should hide

NO grits!!

back she gets
eggs, toast, coffee
as ordered
and. . .grits

NO Grits! he declared,
but gently she shared
"honey" she said,
as southern waitresses do,
"grits is like grace
it comes to you, too
whether you want it or not"

Prevenient

don't use a five-cent word
when you can use one worth a quarter
that's the church's operating order

so prevenient is the church's
description of grace:
it prevails—it takes first place

does that mean that I have to
eat the grits have I no choice
can I resist have I a voice?

The waitress seems to think
I can't resist—I have no choice

hmmm...

but here's a contrary opinion
Jesus tells about a wedding feast
all the guests who were preferred
refused to come so then the least
were brought in—they concurred
except one poor guest
with no proper vest
was harshly ejected
many are invited
but not all are elected*

hmmm...

*Matthew 22:1-14

Weather

Whither the weather we wonder
are weather and climate asunder
weather is measured in ten-day series
while
climate-is-multi-decade-average-weather-properties
a mouth full—so many complexities

news media and their political allies
want our full and rapt attention
blaring headlines catch our eyes
drama guarantees retention

so now we know all is not well
even the UN says we're headed to hell

but UN's own Panel on Climate Change
says it's not so—that there's a range
of factors requiring accounting
with the results amounting
to a calming assurance surmounting
the panic

Climate is changing indeed
as always it has, so heed
the Chicken Little fable –
bring calm reason to the table

Naked Greed

Nakedness embarrasses me
a major law firm declares without shame
recovering billions is their game
ad features woman naked in her greed
more more is her constant creed
I'm embarrassed at her nakedness
and at the firm seeming to profess
only the best of client's interest

yet secretly imagining that I might bring suit
imagining what might I do with all that fruit
oh dear, so greed is also my sin
that woman and I must be kin

the difference is that she has no clothes
I look for fig leaf to cover those
ugly parts of me
nakedness embarrasses me

my leaf a tithe for the common good
then they won't look under my hood
to see the greed that's hidden there

nakedness embarrasses me

The Struggle

how do I combine
the work divine—
bringing justice to the world
removing evil all 'round

with

being fully content
dwelling in the tent
of current perfection
sans future direction

zen master says
do both

The Buddha Paradox

to be rich—be poor
to know—don't
to be active—stop
both—neither

be here now
you contain all

Similar

"they are all assholes"
he says righteously

and he is one of *my kind*
the one who will find
things pretty much like I do
I share his perspective, too

they
are quite disgusting
yet currently the hustings
are their territory

and what is so painful
absolutely baneful
my friend doesn't see
that he is not free

of the same hatefulness
he condemns in them

do you reckon that
if he knew
he shared their condition
it might affect his position?

The Super Blue Moon

Today she told me of
the super blue moon
that we would not soon
see again—fourteen years

so tonight I step outside
there she is so wide
and bright with shiny face
smiling dancing in a place
she's ready to descend from
and come embrace

and welcome us

The Secret

Men are in charge
well. . .by and large
this is patriarchy
we men are stronger
our brains are longer
we know things
we can do things

besides (here's the secret)
we are terrified
we have to dominate
that's why we nominate
ourselves as master
we fear disaster
from that mysterious
intriguing, alluring, secretive, inward
omniscient omni-competent creature
whom we love and hate in equal measure
the one called
woman

Quantum Physics

energy, energy everywhere
and away none will go
energy, energy everywhere
and every particle flow

it may slow down
or it may speed
it will yet abound
and accomplish its deed
of life

energy, energy everywhere

Fall Haiku

Fall and leaves falling
Makes my heart so very glad
Cool and pleasant days

Nakedness Revisited

well maybe it is not always bad
naked limbs—on trees I mean
(the others may be ok too)

late fall afternoon
in my wide-open back yard
I'm sitting and seeing—seeing

one gorgeous healthy tree center
and along the fence the sentinels
who've been there forever
some with naked limbs

sun long hidden from here
setting the tops of the trees
back there on fire

and those naked limbs
for all to see in this bright light
I think they are departing this life
soon to join their sister limb
long since on the ground
in the new incarnation

oh, I see I see
the beauty in those naked tree
limbs I had missed before

is there beauty everywhere?

Shawn

Hanged himself yesterday

I am angry
and sad

that he never let himself be loved
that he never believed he was loved

he died alone

The Heaven I Don't Believe In

wouldn't it be something
if Helen and Shawn met
in the heaven I don't believe in

and she gives him the
warm love she has to give
and he receives it
and is warmed

Quantum Philosophy

yes or no
up or down
in or out
day or night
black or white
positive or negative
right or wrong
this or that

You get the drift

And on one level
it's easy to revel
in the simplicity of

"or"

it is definitely and simply

this OR that

entangled, the quantums say
spin right *and* spin left
positive charge *and* negative true
matter *and* antimatter too
endless energy continuous span
it's never or it's always and

positive and negative both true

Other Ways

right and wrong exist too
good and evil in me and you
always tense marriage between the two

but they are married
for all eternity
and so are you

East and West

Is it too simple to say
that east says be
and west says do

probably

He and She

she sees it all
comments gently
occasional blunt

he sees little
often blunt
occasional gentle

is that too simple too?

Dumbass

the man goes to his office
insurance broker, pastor, lawyer
he goes to his office
that's what the man does
the man goes to his office

this man young newly wed
he's home for lunch and after
she says, 'let's go to bed'
his father's there, horrified
"get to work, son!"
and so he complied
the man goes to his office

dumbass

Peace

Who am I who are you
do you wonder that too

I once told my theology prof
"I am wonderful"
he seemed offended
and made some derogation

I was hurt and surprised
Psalm said I was wonderful
how could the professor
not know that

yet more regularly
I know my faults and
my sin is ever before me
(Psalm says that too)

that's why I resist
and so firmly insist
on the falsity of dualism
and the truth of monism

I am wonderful and hateful
I am fearfully and wonderfully made
also says the Psalm
I can do good and I can do evil
in equal measure

Peace

a silly question I guess
I ask it nevertheless
how do I live in this confusion
Paul asked for deliverance
instead I seek acceptance
of the being that I am

and peace

Spoiler alert: you might want to read *Horse* by Geraldine Brooks before you read this poem

Connection

a beautiful poem by a Black poet
a wonderful novel by a white woman
both assaulted my feeling fortress

to paraphrase NASA
we have cognition
I have read and grasp
the evil and pain of slavery
and its lingering aftermath
I re-cognize the concepts

the poet describes living daily
with the fear
his sons leave the house
never to return

the woman combines
story of son in 1850
being sold away from home
intertwines a 2019 aftermath

Black man leaves his sweetheart
for a run in the park
and never returns
mistaken for a rapist
he is shot and killed

each so powerfully expressed

Connection

I didn't think it
cognition not operative
I felt it
I cried

am, I "appropriating" feelings
I cannot claim to have
when my visceral response
to those artists is

I knew when he left to run
that he would not be back
I knew it
I know the poet's fear
that they won't return
I know it

because

I know the thrill of feeling
whenever one of mine
drives out of the driveway
that they will not return
a wreck on the highway.

The Dog that Did Not Bark

many thousand years ago
Abram left his father
saying god told him to go
to the land of milk and honey
promised him new real estate
his own domain—no other state

did god forget or just not care
that the philistines were already there
some say winners write the story
explaining things to enhance their glory

one thing seems sure
in this I am secure
Philistines and Israelites
were all Canaanites
who engaged in constant fights
for many thousand years

is this just another instance
of standard human circumstance
Cain and Abel writ large
who is to be in charge

where in the world has it failed
to be the pattern that prevailed
human nature from the start
enough to break our hardest heart

The Dog that Did Not Bark

Sherlock Holmes was said to remark
about the dog that did not bark
a remarkable fact it seems to me:
in our basic book we only see
scant evidence of gods decree
that negotiation is to be
the norm for our behavior

thus once again we may conclude
there is no god who will intrude

Watson says to Sherlock
you fail to notice that
both Isaiah and Sermon on the Mount
call for making peace, so then. . .

are Pinker Ridley and Rosling right
is our human tendency to fight
gradually declining so that instead
we're slowly learning to break bread
and talk?

they don't contradict
what you suggest

rather they propose
that it is up to us
and t'was ever thus

it is up to us you see
it's called human agency

Poetry

you are a poet
and I claim to be also
let's play together

A Funny Thing Happened on the Way

If you sign up to be an official of the organization, it probably behooves you to know what that organization believes and how it operates. (Note to self: for a long time you didn't let yourself recognize that what it says it believes and how it behaves may be contradictory.) Since I was a designated officer of said organization, I spent many years of my life trying to incorporate its beliefs and practices into my very core. This required me to try to make sense of the rather elaborate and complex theory it had developed about itself over many years. A slightly cynical person might also note that another motivating factor is that this organization credentialed me and paid my salary (plus benefits).

Did I really believe the theory? Even now that is hard for me to answer. I can say that I tried hard to make sense of it, and I succeeded in part if not completely for a long time.

Of course, as a "young turk", as we called ourselves as a cohort in our early days as fellow junior officers of the organization, I could be quite flippant in my clever critiques of the older leaders somewhat above us in the hierarchy and their rather antiquated ways of describing the organization and practicing its ways.

I can't say exactly what has happened to this long-held loyalty; maybe it is enough to say that at heart I'm a good boy who respects authority; it seems that my earnest efforts to truly understand the theories and practices from 'inside' so to speak, have gradually—very gradually—led me to the understanding that they are, literally, absurd. Yet the organization continues to exist. What's going on?

I penned a little whimsical poem recently about a fish:

Fish

A Parable

take a lesson from the fish

old joke
what does the fish in the lake say
when he runs into the concrete barrier

DAM

ok that's out of the way
now how do you convince the fish
that he lives in a particular atmosphere

tell him maybe. . .but
he'll just say, compared to what?
Air, you might say
what's that? he'd say
I don't believe you, he'd say
this is the only atmosphere there is

do you have to take him out
to convince him

and can he survive if you do

Darwin says that it took
countless generations for the fish
to adapt to land-living

FISH

yes but one fish to lead the way
you might say

there's good news here to see
it is that we are free
to explore many atmospheres
in water air rocks oxygen adheres

Mortal

a good many storms
during her long life
some beyond norms
potentially rife with danger
there were seasons
of scarcity and of abundance
of ease and of turbulence

she was sturdy and solid
she doesn't much like the word
but phlegmatic
describes her temperament

the wind could blow pretty hard
bend limbs send leaves swirling
that had happened many times
but for the most part
she maintained her calm

she was now mature
a good long life
then
a storm like she'd never
felt before struck her
and she was disturbed
to her very roots

it didn't happen this time
but now I know, she said
I could be taken down

Life

five hundred years—that's as nothing
two thousand rings—that's something
life persists

Gift

My son and family live some distance
from where I am, so I see them
seldom
for all that, each visit is a gift
especially the twins

recently returned from a wonderful
five days I've been trying to express
beautifully poetically movingly
in my new-found medium

my delight in that family
especially the twins

but the poetry does not flow
I tried images of strangeness
morphing into my awareness
of our common humanity
and I tried images of
opening a gift with
"some assembly required"
which led me to images of a flower
gradually opening to reveal
its beauty
especially the twins

I do marvel at the patience
in the everydayness of
the care required

Gift

and given by parents and siblings

and for myself rejoicing at
the gift—the twins each
revealing ever so gradually
her unique being
residing so deeply hidden
in their mute but not silent
awkward dance

starkly revealing how different
we are—each from the other
strangers
they are significantly 'delayed'
physically and mentally

each of us is stranger to the other
they have a language all their own
unknown to me and yet
I get up close and see
they are just like me
one the same

ol blue-eyed Frank had his say
he declared, "I did it my way"
so they

do it their way as do I
living what they're given
as we all must

in the midst of one another
sister brother father mother

family

Other Ways

they give us grief and we them
they give us joy and we them
they give us life and we them

they are we and we are them
strangers and also one

family

how can that be
they don't know
neither do I
but it is so

thanks for the gift
especially the twins

The Horror

November 10, 2023

she was maybe three
running naked down the road
wide-eyed terror
mouth open soundless cry
which you cannot fail to hear
napalmed flesh

do you remember that photograph?

last night I watched and tonight the same
I can barely stand it
I force myself turn on the news
see the face, blood running down
hear her wail the death of
her mother
her father
her brother

STOP!
I don't want to see this
but I must

I will not go to
israel/palestine/gaza/west bank
but I must attend
these are my kin

Mink

Each evening at my bedtime
my devotional for the day
is one poem by Mary Oliver

last night I read *Mink*
twice
my breathing stops

my god that's beautiful
in its innocent simplicity

it's about nothing

it's about everything

Three Red Tomatoes

Beautifully formed deliciously red
They sat in the grocery store
On impulse I bought them

I'll cook up a hamburger
and put on a slice or two
fanciful I almost never
cook a hamburger

so I put them in the windowsill
where they sat
some time later they began
to sprout like potatoes

so yesterday I threw them
out into the field
earth to earth
dust to dust
life to life

TS Eliot Revisited

she is large
it is not her size I reference
it is very definitely her presence
she gave me a charge
and rapt my attention
as none has before

we've been casual friends
and work colleagues
for several years
this was an intense
and powerful encounter
like none before

she is black I am white
we discussed two black students
known to her not to me
I'll be overseeing their
educational process soon

recently one described as very bright
was captioned as "arrogant" by
a mentor

incensed voice blazing eyes gives some sense
of the demeanor with which
she told me of this appellation

not loud, yet it felt so

TS Eliot Revisited

"you have no idea
what it is to be black
to be seen as
and called arrogant
this multi-accomplished
very bright graduate student

"you have no idea."

Well, yes, I do have an idea
I've read—I 'know'
but knowing is not the issue
her gift to me that day
was her trust in me and
the power of the passion
not the 'facts'

I felt it from her
and so knew it
in a new way

I have been here before
I'm conversant with the facts
I've heard them
but I know it again . . .

for the first time.

Meeting

student clergy in hospital
learning to make human contact
start to practice, and in fact
soon discover that
they are in a

dynamic bidirectional relationship
(I love how academics talk)

Id est (I can do academics, see?)
I have an effect on the patient
the patient has an effect on me
we are connected . . . in a
dynamic bidirectional relationship

How it All Started

Joseph may have been spoiled
Daddy loved him above all others
but later all could see
he was the genius he claimed to be
he could predict and make happen

little Joe bragged, he dreamed
my sheaf of wheat stood tall
eleven others bowed low
my star shone bright
all the others bowed so

the brothers all—except Reuben
want to kill him
they throw him in a deep well
holding him to sell
to a merchant band
Reuben is dismayed
the only adult in the land

enter—as always in this Book—
deus ex machina so-called
who intervenes—now look
he interprets the Pharoah's dreams
and becomes minister prime
of all Egypt. It was his time.

When the predicted famine comes
it envelopes Canaan, too
so Jacob sends the boys down

Other Ways

to buy supplies in Egypt town

Joseph knows them right away
In time, I'm your brother
he reveals, then to allay
their fears he chants the song
the *deus* has planned it all along

and the *deus* is not done
he also arranges for dad
all the brothers
and all the others to
inhabit the best real estate
in Egypt

furthermore
deus promises Jacob
that they will one day
return to their rightful
homeland Canaan
the promised land

And so they did
Moses leading the way

'twas ever thus
the Hebrew children
boast the land god-given
the other one—Hagar's offspring
cry out with anguish riven
god says we're a great nation too

five thousand years
internecine war
is there to be more?

where is brother Reuben?

How It Ends

cynical or just cold
I make so bold
to say how it ends

take your pick
Palestinian-Israeli conflict
Or Ukraine-Russian

oh, no specifics here
fires burn hot
and then not
ashes left
and coals

do these end some day
some way?

Hamas leaders all dead
Israel the victor
or
vice versa
or
same with Russia/Ukraine
or
truce, negotiated peace
thirty-eighth parallel
or
one side "wins"
the other defeated

Other Ways

fire is out?

my brother tells about a spider
a story with much wider
meaning—the arachnid was
crawling across the floor
he did not know the poor
creature was pregnant.

death to her by his big foot
surprise
scooting everywhere
baby spiders all over
alive

mama dies
yet
life doesn't wane
coals smolder
then spring into
flame

damn resurrection
it's part of the plot
whether you believe in it
or not

www.ingramcontent.com/pod-product-compliance
Lightning Source LLC
Chambersburg PA
CBHW071715040426
42446CB00011B/2067